REAL WORLD ECONOMICS ™

How Venture Capital Works

Peter K. Ryan

ROSEN
PUBLISHING®

New York

Special thanks to my parents, Peter and Carol, for giving me a wonderful and blessed life, and to my brother, Chris, and sister, Emily, for their lifelong support.

Published in 2013 by The Rosen Publishing Group, Inc.
29 East 21st Street, New York, NY 10010

Copyright © 2013 by The Rosen Publishing Group, Inc.

First Edition

Library of Congress Cataloging-in-Publication Data

Ryan, Peter K.
How venture capital works/Peter K. Ryan.—1st ed.
    p. cm. —(Real world economics)
Includes bibliographical references and index.
ISBN 978-1-4488-6786-8 (library binding)
1. Venture capital. I. Title.
HG4751.R93 2013
332'.04154—dc23

                                                                2011045416

Manufactured in the United States of America

CPSIA Compliance Information: Batch #S12YA: For further information, contact Rosen Publishing, New York, New York, at 1-800-237-9932.

Contents

INTRODUCTION

Mark Zuckerberg founded Facebook in his dorm room at Harvard in October 2003 while only a sophomore in college. It began as an idea, a place to chat, share pictures, and socialize. Today it has over 750 million users worldwide. How did Mark Zuckerberg's idea grow from a dorm room in Massachusetts to multiple offices around the world employing thousands of people and generating billions of dollars in annual revenue? The answer is venture capital financing.

Zuckerberg started Facebook with loans from friends and family, but in order for his idea to grow to its full potential, he raised a much larger amount of money from venture capital investors. In a series of investments made by an angel investor, two venture capital firms, and Microsoft Corporation in 2004 and 2007, Facebook was able to hire the employees, equipment, and office space needed to launch Facebook onto the world stage. These funds gave Facebook the opportunity to turn its ideas and ambitions into reality.

Venture capitalists, such as Todd MacLean of Accel Partners, provide start-up companies with money, expertise, experience, and access to networks of people who can positively influence the success of a start-up.

The Facebook story is one of many start-ups that owes its successes to the venture capital industry. Venture capital is money that is invested in risky companies in return for partial ownership of the company. Venture capital is provided by venture capitalists (VCs) and venture capital firms. Because of venture capital we have many technologies and products that we take for granted today, such as microchips, computers, Facebook, and the Internet itself.

The venture capital industry is made up of many firms throughout the world whose purpose is to find new companies (start-ups) that need money to grow into successful businesses. The venture capital investor is given ownership of a percentage of a company in return for the investment. Over time, if the start-up succeeds, the company will either be bought by another company, issue shares to the public in an IPO (initial public offering), or become large and profitable enough to pay back the investment. If successful, the VC will earn a return many times greater than the initial investment.

Venture capitalists serve a very important role in our society by helping to bring to fruition ideas and technologies that improve the quality of life for all people. Technology and medicine in particular have benefited enormously from venture capital. Advances and breakthroughs in disease treatment and medical devices have been made by companies that have received venture funding.

This book explores and discusses the venture capital process and all the people involved in it to help us understand what venture capital is, why a start-up would want to accept venture capital, and why venture capital is an important part of our economy.

CHAPTER ONE
UNDERSTANDING START-UPS

A start-up is an infant company. All companies that exist go through a start-up phase as they mature, but not all companies that start up will survive.

Start-ups are created by a founder or a group of founders who come together with an idea and form a company in order to make their idea real. The founders create a legal business entity, which is made up of shares of ownership in the company. In the case of a single founder, he or she would own 100 percent of the company. In the case of two or more founders, they would split the ownership of the company however they decided. Those shares of ownership are very important because they represent the degree of control and interest. Control is the right to make decisions about the company. Interest is the right to the financial value of the company.

CREATING VALUE

Start-up companies usually have limited resources. There is often little cash available to hire employees or to pay the founders a salary. Whatever money is available is usually used to develop the product or service that the founders envision, and very little is ever wasted.

It may take years for the founders of a company to create a product that works or a technology that is viable, or to develop a service that is valuable. During that period when the founders are inventing and turning ideas into reality, they are rarely paid a salary. Their only compensation is the ownership of the company and the hope that their work will be valuable in the future.

At some point during the start-up phase, a company will reach a point when it needs capital (money) to invest in the development of its product or service. The first places that most start-ups look for money are family and friends. They are usually the most likely people to make an investment. This initial funding is called seed capital, so named because the company will hopefully grow from this seed investment. This seed money sustains the company until the team is able to develop its idea into reality.

If all goes well, the company will survive the initial start-up phase, create a real product or service, and sell that product or service for a profit. The founders may then be finally rewarded with salaries and will be able to realize the value of their shares in the company. They may then claim the reward of all their risk. This concept is called risk versus reward. The more anyone is willing to risk on an endeavor, the greater the potential reward. In the case of a start-up, the founders may risk everything they have to make their company succeed, and if successful their reward can be enormous.

Y Combinator

There are many angel investment firms, and Y Combinator is one of the premier firms worldwide. Y Combinator is a very unusual firm in that it chooses a large number of firms to invest in each year, each investment being no more than $20,000.

It brings all of the companies it invests in to its campus in Silicon Valley for three months where the founders work on their start-ups under the guidance of the Y Combinator group. Many different start-ups work simultaneously and interact with others to stimulate new and better ideas. Y Combinator usually receives only 2 to 10 percent equity in the companies in which it invests, but it provides support and guidance for the life of the company.

Y Combinator represents a new model of venture investing that uses networking and social interaction as a means to stimulate companies to grow faster and better through the natural forces of learning and interacting.

The Ownership Structure

There are limited ways for founders or investors to profit from their investment. This is why the type of company ownership becomes important. Start-ups are usually purchased by larger established companies, go public on stock exchanges, or remain private and continue to grow over time. In each case the founders and the initial investors will be repaid based upon how much of the company they own.

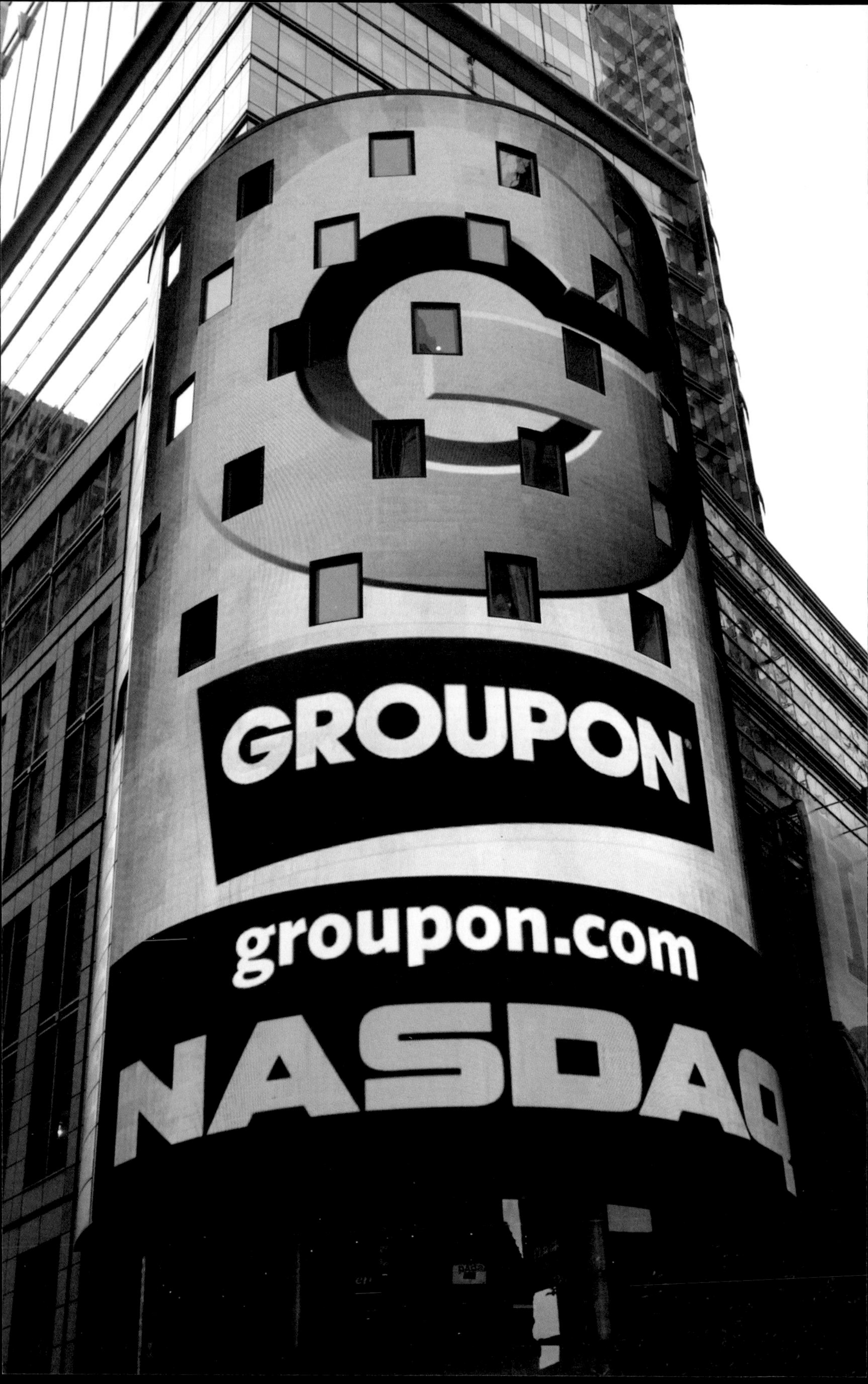
GROUPON
groupon.com
NASDAQ

If the start-up is purchased by another company the total purchase price will be divided up between all the shareholders. If the company sells its shares to the general public in an IPO, all shareholders will be able to sell their shares to people outside the company for a profit or loss. If the company continues to grow and profit, the shareholders will be paid dividends, or pieces of the annual profit, for as long as they own the shares.

Because of the limitations on when and how investors can get their money out of a start-up, the expectation is that the return will be very high. In most cases, venture capital is secured in a start-up for three to seven years. However, the percentage of start-ups that succeed beyond three years is small. Therefore, investors expect to receive a large portion of ownership in the company for the investment. The investors can demand a large ownership stake because the venture is naturally risky. There are many other safe investments that they can make instead of the start-up. Other areas in which investors could put their money are stocks, bonds, mutual funds, and other more common assets.

Who Invests in Start-Ups?

Investing in a start-up is not at all like investing in a stock or a bond. Stock and bond traders can buy and sell their investments at any time. This is because stocks and bonds trade in markets in which many other investors are willing to buy and sell, making it easy to get into and out of an investment. If you

In 2011, Groupon was one of the most watched private companies in the world. In 2010, the company turned down a $6 billion buyout offer from Google with the hope that it would make more money in an IPO.

The requirements for listing a company on the NYSE are very strict, such as having to have an IPO market value of at least $40 million.

purchase a stock, you can sell that stock right away. Investors in start-up companies are involved in what is an all-or-none investment, meaning that they will either get all of their money back plus a big profit if the company succeeds, or they may get nothing because the company may fail.

Rewards have to be appropriate to the risk of the investment, which is why there are very few venture capital investors, and why there are many stock and bond investors—venture capital is generally a much more risky investment than stocks and bonds.

Regardless of where they choose to put their money, investors are all looking for the same thing: return. Return is the amount of money that investors gets back on top of their initial investment. For example, if investor A invests $100 into a stock, and it provides a 10 percent return, investor A gets its original $100 back plus an additional $10 (10 percent of $100) for a return of $10. Investor B invests $100 into a start-up and it provides a 500 percent return. Investor B gets its original $100 plus a return of $500. Although investor B made much more money than investor A, investor B may have been exposed to much more risk than investor A, and it was very possible that the return could have been negative 100 percent.

A START-UP NAMED GOOGLE

The theory behind venture capital and return on investment can best be understood when explored in the context of a real company. Google is a technology that most people use every day. It began as an idea and a passion shared between its two founders, Larry Page and Sergey Brin. Both were graduate students at Stanford University at the time that they started the company, and they had very little money to start the company with.

Sergey Brin (*left*) and Larry Page, the founders of Google, are among the most notable and successful entrepreneurs of the last twenty years.

Over the course of several years, Page and Brin worked tirelessly on their first version of the Google search engine. They used every bit of free hardware they could find, brought in several unpaid team members who took stock in lieu of pay, and they bootstrapped, or conserved money, to achieve an initial product launch. Within a few weeks of publicly launching Google, it quickly became so popular that their servers were completely overwhelmed, forcing Page and Brin to consider the importance of raising money to pay for additional programmers and many more servers.

In August 1998, Google took an initial round of angel investment from a veteran computer industry executive named Andy Bechtolsheim. One year later Google took an investment of $25 million from a pair of venture investment firms, Sequoia Capital and Kleiner, Perkins, Caufield and Byers. Google used the money to hire the best computer scientists and systems engineers it could find, and it invested heavily in computers, servers, and network infrastructure. Google went public in an initial public offering on August 25, 2004, raising $1.2 billion in additional capital, and generating a market cap (the total value of all the shares in existence) of $23 billion.

CHAPTER TWO

THE ROLE OF VENTURE CAPITAL

Imagine for a moment that you have a great idea for a new kind of product unlike anything that has existed before, but one that you are sure can have a huge impact on people's lives and will probably make you a good deal of money. How would you go about making that product and getting it into stores for people to buy?

For starters, you would need to develop the product. You would have to experiment with different prototypes and models, and after a lot of trial and error, you would arrive at a final product concept. Then you would need to figure out how to make that product in large quantities, probably requiring manufacturing equipment and employees. You would also need people to help you advertise and market your product and folks to make sure that all the products shipped out to the stores for sale.

Venture capital firms often get involved with the strategic leadership of the companies in which they invest. Their staff often provides expertise and skills that help start-ups improve their operations.

That's a lot of work, and it would require a good deal of money. If you spent a lot of time brainstorming and planning you could probably come up with a very accurate estimate of how much money you would need. The problem is, who would be willing to give you the money to do it?

GETTING MONEY

Start-up companies usually try to get their initial funding from any source they can find. Many founders will use their personal savings and may even have full-time jobs while they build their company. Many start-ups will begin with almost no money, forcing the founders to be very creative in order to make things happen. The spirit of entrepreneurship is what enables start-up founders to make it past the initial hurdles of starting a business where others would normally fail. However, even the cleverest of founders will hit a point at which they must find a source of funding in order to move from one phase of a business to the next.

Family and Friends

Many start-up companies get their first outside funding from their family and friends. They are the most likely to believe in the founders ideas and ability to succeed, even if the idea is very ambitious. Family and friends are usually willing to take a chance on a start-up because they have faith and trust in the founders. Usually the amount of money that can be raised by friends and family is limited. The agreement between a friend or family investor and the start-up can be informal, but there is usually a promise of equity.

Angels

Once a start-up has grown to this proof-of-concept stage, it can pursue a kind of investor known as an angel investor, who may make a generous investment without taking too much in return. There are many angel investors in the United States and around the world. The leading angel investment firms will pool the resources of many individual angel investors for the sake of creating a larger fund and to provide a better balance of skills and talents to help start-ups succeed. A great example of

Paul Graham, a partner at innovative venture capital firm Y Combinator, enables start-ups to work directly with seasoned and successful entrepreneurs in a very intimate and supportive environment.

the current angel investment community is Y Combinator, an angel firm that has several successful start-ups in development now and has several notable start-ups that have graduated to the next stage of growth.

Angel investors have earned the term "angel" because they tend to lend money to start-ups very early on, often before a proof-of-concept can be seen, at a time when a lot of faith and trust is required on the part of the investor. Angel investors want to see start-ups succeed for altruistic reasons in addition to the hope for a return on their investment. However, in most cases, an angel investor is likely to provide funding to start-ups based upon terms that are often not very demanding or restrictive of the start-up. Angels make it possible for many companies to make the leap from a garage or a basement to an office or a warehouse, turning their ideas from hobby to profession.

Venture Capital Firms

Once angel funding is exhausted, it is time for a start-up to turn to venture capitalists for funding. VCs demand a high price for their funding. Unlike friends and family and angel investors, VCs expect an unusually high return on their investment. VCs expect to make many multiples of their investment to consider funding a start-up. VCs will require a substantial portion of ownership of the company in return for their capital, along with voting rights and limited control of the company. Ownership and control are very high prices to pay for funding, which is why start-ups must very carefully consider taking money from a VC.

Working with Venture Capitalists

VCs offer several valuable resources to start-up companies. First they provide more capital than a bank would ever consider or an angel could ever provide. VCs also provide expertise in the areas of management, marketing, operations, and other business capabilities that many start-up companies lack. VCs bring access to extremely valuable networks of expertise and talent, which can be utilized for a variety of purposes. Finally, VCs provide start-up companies with a kind of "stamp of approval" that gives the start-up credibility in the eyes of the world.

Accepting venture capital is usually a very large decision for a start-up to make. Start-up founders have to give up both shares and control in exchange for funding. Many entrepreneurs try to hold off from taking venture capital as long as possible, and some try to avoid taking venture capital at all. The challenge that start-ups face is finding investors who are willing to take on the kind of risk that a start-up represents. There aren't many banks or private investors who are both willing and able to make investment in risky start-ups. Venture capital firms are staffed by people with a wide range of educations and backgrounds, enabling them to bring real tangible skills to the start-up. They fill the gap that banks leave and provide the funding that start-ups need. Banks don't typically have expertise in specific hands-on business and technical management.

In order to understand why venture capital exists, the concept of risk and reward needs to be understood. Risk, in a financial sense, is exposure to the effects of external factors

Some successful entrepreneurs, such as Marc Andreessen (*left*), become venture capitalists later in their careers. Their entrepreneurial spirit combined with the right connections gives them a competitive advantage.

beyond your control. VCs put their money at risk when they invest in start-ups. The start-up could fail and the entire investment that the VC made could vanish overnight. In order for the investor to make an investment with great risk, there must be a very large potential reward, meaning that the investment has to have a very large payout to justify the risk. So a high-risk investment must have a big potential reward, and a low-risk investment requires only a low potential reward.

Understanding Risk

Venture capitalists are a unique kind of investor because they choose to invest in the most risky possible businesses. They take on enormous risk with each start-up investment, but they also take on the potential for enormous returns with each start-up investment. A VC may invest a few million dollars in a start-up, and if that start-up succeeds the investment could be worth many times that initial investment amount.

There are other much less risky ways to invest money, the stock market being one of the first choices. Why would people choose to put their money in venture capital when they could put their money in the less risky stock market? The most basic reason is that most stock investors are satisfied with a rate of return of between 5 to 15 percent, whereas a VC is more interested in a rate of return of upward of 500 percent.

Webvan

What's a Webvan? During the peak of the dot-com Internet bubble, one of the most glaringly overvalued and overhyped companies that received venture funding was Webvan. The concept of Webvan was simple: customers could purchase groceries from a

wide selection online, and Webvan would deliver the customers' purchases to their doors within thirty minutes.

In its initial stages, it did very well with customers who loved having groceries delivered right to their door, and over time Webvan added more and more items to its inventory. At some point Webvan needed to expand into massive warehouses to accommodate it all, and management determined it needed to invest heavily in building new high-tech, state-of-the-art distribution centers near major cities to handle their projected customer growth. The estimate is that Webvan spent $1 billion on warehouses. However, Webvan's management team and venture investors grossly overestimated the potential market size and invested far too heavily in buildings that it couldn't use and inventory that it couldn't sell.

Webvan was founded in 1999, and by 2001 it was bankrupt. Webvan represented the collective frenzy at the peak of the dot-com bubble. Venture capital investors were so eager to be part of the dot-com moneymaking machine that they overlooked common sense and due diligence in favor of hype and high-profile branding.

When Webvan closed its doors in 2001, all of its equipment was sold off to pay back its investors.

Equity and Company Ownership

When a VC invests in a company, the form of investment is usually a type of equity that provides the VC with a wide range of protections, insurance, and guarantees. Ultimately, investors want to see their money grow about five times over the course of five to six years. This goal requires a "liquidity event," which means that the start-up company is purchased by another company, it goes public via an IPO, or the management team of the start-up buys the company back from the venture investors. This liquidity event is necessary for the venture investors to get their money back. Without a liquidity event, venture investors can end up owning shares of the start-up for a very long time and not having access to their cash investment.

Dilution and Shares Outstanding

To protect their investment, venture investors have over the years created a set of standard practices and agreements, which are widely used by most venture investing professionals. There are specific types of shares that VCs prefer because they provide the best protection in the event of a bad outcome and the maximum return in the event of a good outcome.

These shares are called convertible preferred equity shares. There are clauses that are added to the agreement that dictate various actions based upon possible trigger events that can occur. There is also a very strict method and terminology used for valuing start-up companies, which all venture investors use. These standard practices make it possible for the venture investing community and the start-up community to have

26

a common language and frame of reference upon which to evaluate deals and make reasoned decisions possible.

VALUING A START-UP

When a VC wants to invest in a company it must first determine what the value of the start-up is. This can be very difficult, especially when the start-up is in the process of creating a new product or concept that may not exist yet, making it difficult to

Pets.com was among the most notable dot-com stories. Its Web site looked very much like major online retailers today, but because of bad timing and poor financial decisions, the company failed.

value. In order to make the valuation possible, venture capitalists use sophisticated financial models. However, much of the valuation process is estimation and assumption based on best-effort analysis of possible outcomes. So one VC valuation of a company may be different than the valuation of a different VC firm.

Once VCs have determined a value, they next have to determine how much money they should invest. This is not easy because VCs have to lend enough money for the start-up to succeed, but not so much money that the VC's return on investment is lower than they are allowed to seek. This analysis creates two different valuations of the company, the pre-money and the post-money valuation, which allow the VCs to determine what percentage of the company they should own if they invest in the start-up.

A common occurrence is for start-ups to go through multiple rounds of investment, often taking money from different VC groups through a series of different funding events. These are called investment rounds, and each round of investment brings more cash to the company, at the cost of ownership and control. Shares of the company are "diluted" in value with each additional round of funding, and most commonly the first venture capitalists in will have protections to prevent their shares from diluting. If you think of the ownership of the company in terms of a pie chart, dilution means that your piece of the pie gets smaller.

MYTHS and FACTS

MYTH Venture capitalists want to take control of every aspect of the business.

FACT Venture capital investors know that trying to have too much control can disturb the culture and normal operations of a company and can have negative impacts on morale, passion, and leadership.

MYTH When you sign with a venture capitalist, you are giving away all your hard earned equity.

FACT Venture capital investors do require a substantial amount of equity for their investment, but it is only as much as is needed to provide the necessary funding and nothing more.

MYTH Angel investors don't expect to make as much money as venture capitalists, so it's better to take only angel money.

FACT Angel investors are willing to be the helping hand to start the start-up on a path to success, but just like every other investor, they expect to get their fair share.

CHAPTER THREE

THE VALUE OF VENTURE CAPITAL

Venture capital firms bring other forms of value to start-up companies in addition to their capital investment. A venture firm may have expertise in a particular industry. Venture firms also have access to networks of people and talent that they can use to help a start-up progress. These additional resources are often critically important to the success of a start-up. Many start-up companies are founded by young and inexperienced people, who may not have the skills or training to run a business after it grows beyond a certain size. By bringing in outside expertise and guidance, the VC firm can help the start-up get past hurdles and continue to grow.

BOARD OVERSIGHT

All start-ups have a management team, the people who run the company on a day-to-day basis. Start-ups that take VC investments will also have a board of directors that oversees the management team. The management team has the power to make decisions on behalf of the company, and the board of directors has the power to determine if the management team is acting in the best interests of the company. It's a balance of power to prevent any one person or group from acting recklessly.

Venture capital investors always ensure that they have some form of oversight and control over a company once they have invested in it. Usually the venture capitalist will require a position on the start-up's board of directors as a term in the investment deal. With a seat on the board, the venture investor will be actively engaged in the long-term guidance and direction of the company. This seat on the board of directors

The board of directors of companies, both new and old, meet on a regular basis with executives to review performance, strategy, and business plan.

gives the venture investor the ability to encourage and support the success of the start-up and also helps the venture investor to protect its investment by making sure that everyone in the company is doing what they are supposed to do and to ensure that the company is always working toward a successful outcome.

MANAGEMENT SUPPORT

Venture investors will often coach start-up founders and companies to help improve the overall performance of the founders and the business. Venture investors have a lot of exposure to many start-up companies and see many common problems and successes across all of them. That knowledge gives venture investors unique insight and awareness of behaviors that foster success and behaviors that encourage failure.

NETWORKING

Perhaps the most important additional benefit that venture investment firms bring to start-ups is access to networks of experts, influencers, investors, and other prominent people. When highly regarded groups of people take notice of a start-up and are able to have contact with the management team, there is a much better chance that the start-up will gain the credibility it needs with investment bankers, large corporations, and governments. This is very important because at the end of the three- to seven-year window that venture investors target for their start-up investments the company has to have a liquidity event. Access to the right people makes the likelihood of that liquidity event much greater.

TURNING IDEAS INTO REALITY

Although venture investors are motivated by profit and their primary concern is ensuring a successful outcome for all of their investments, they also serve a valuable role for society by enabling inventors to turn their ideas into reality. Venture investors serve a role similar to that of a scout. They look for promising new companies and technologies that have the potential to succeed in the marketplace. This activity fosters the introduction of products and services that have a large net benefit on many more people than just the VC and the start-up company. Without venture investment we would not have the Microsoft Windows operating system, Apple computers,

There are countless components in Apple's innovative tablet computer, the iPad. The glass, microchips, storage devices, and more are all produced by innovative young companies, which were likely backed by venture capital.

or microprocessors. The list of technologies that have benefitted from the activity of venture capital investment is very long.

Venture Capital Abroad

Although most U.S.-based VCs may jokingly say no, there are in fact VCs in countries around the world. The style of investing and appetite for risk is very different in most places, and geographic boundaries tend to make VCs behave according to the culture of their locale. Europe has a lot of venture capital activity, but it tends to be very conservative and aim for long-term investments in late-stage companies that already have proven success. China and India have tremendous venture capital activity, and some would suggest that the real opportunities for VC success are in India and China. There are hotspots around the world where VC funding is picking up, places such as Eastern Europe, Brazil, North Africa, Colombia, and Southeast Asia. Each region has its own flavor of VC investing, but they are all looking for the same thing: the next big company.

From Idea to Invention

Another purpose that venture investors serve is to link the basic scientific research and development done at universities, private research facilities, and government facilities with the marketplace. Many scientists work on technologies in a very abstract

Patents, such as this one that inventor Thomas Edison filed for the lightbulb in 1880, are crucial to the innovative spirit of America because they protect the hard work and ingenuity of inventors.

T. A. EDISON.
Electric-Lamp.

No. 223,898.   **Patented Jan. 27, 1880.**

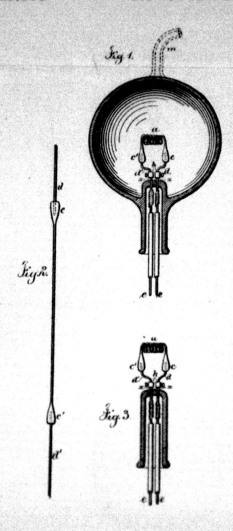

Inventor

Thomas A. Edison

pr Lemuel W. Serrell

Witnesses

Chas. H. Smith

Geo. T. Pinckney

and narrow way. Their research is very focused, and their perspective on their work is very limited. Venture capital investors have the ability to see how inventions and patents can be commercialized. Commercialization is the process of turning an idea or concept into a product or service that can be bought or sold. This is a very important benefit to society because it allows very specific scientific discoveries to be used for the benefit of many people.

START-UP MANIA

When a new technological trend or a period of prosperity occurs, it is common to see many start-up companies form, virtually overnight, to pursue success and fortune. This is called a trend, and the last major start-up trend occurred in the late 1990s during the infancy of the Internet. Hundreds of start-ups formed across the country and around the world all focused on delivering services, software, and solutions using the Internet. This period of frenzied start-up activity was followed by a period of rapid initial public offerings on stock exchanges, referred to as the dot-com bubble.

The dot-com bubble saw the rise and fall of many start-up companies, some which offered valuable solutions and services. Others, when viewed in hindsight, didn't make good financial sense. The fever of a bubble afflicts everyone involved, from the start-up founders all the way up to the venture investors. Many people believe

that the bubble will never burst and that everyone will get rich. Unfortunately, like all financial bubbles, the dot-com bubble burst and caused a lot of people to return to more realistic investment principles and strategies.

During the stock market bubble of the late '90s, the world was swept up in the stock market's dramatic rise. When the market crashed, however, much of its gains were wiped away virtually overnight.

During this wave of technology and venture investing, start-up companies tended to appear almost overnight. One start-up had an idea, raised money, and released a product, which stimulated other start-ups to have ideas, raise money, and release competing products. Competition between start-ups made it more difficult for individual companies to stand out, which made it easier for VCs to pick the companies they thought had the best chance of success.

Raising Money

When funding rounds take place, multiple venture investors can participate at the same time. This means that multiple different investors pool their money into a single sum, which lowers the risk for all investors and provides the start-up with the amount of money it needs to continue progressing.

In some situations, a start-up company may have an idea that is so good and the potential for success so great that multiple venture investors may compete to make the investment. Venture investment firms will try to convince the start-up that they are the best investor for the start-up based on the non-financial benefits that they bring to the table.

Ten Great Questions
to Ask a Venture Capitalist

1 How do you know when you are ready to take money from an angel investor?

2 What do you need to show an angel investor or a VC in order to get their attention?

3 How do you know which VC firm is the right one for your company?

4 What is the best way to approach the valuation negotiation with a VC?

5 Once you've taken on VC investment funds, does the company's culture change?

6 How many companies have you invested in?

7 How many of your companies have been successful?

8 What types of companies do you invest in?

9 Can you give me an example of your typical interactions with the teams of the companies you invest in?

10 Other than money, how do you help young companies in ways that they can't aid themselves?

CHAPTER FOUR

SUCCESSES, FAILURES... AND LESSONS

I n order to better understand what an investment bubble is, one can look at the successes and failures of the dot-com frenzy. This chapter will look at Amazon.com as an example of a successful venture-backed start-up, and at Pets.com as an example of a failed venture-backed start-up. Looking at the differences between the companies' products and services along with the key decisions they made will show how it was possible for one to succeed while the other failed.

AMAZON.COM

In 1994 Jeff Bezos founded Amazon.com as an online bookstore. Within months it also started selling CDs and DVDs. Over time, Amazon added more and more products to its catalog, offering a customer the ability to shop for almost anything at one Web site.

Amazon.com founder Jeff Bezos has revolutionized both the book business and selling products online.

Amazon.com is now a household name. It is one of the most used online shopping destinations in the world. Amazon sells everything from sneakers to computers. It has millions of customers and has dozens of regional distribution centers around the globe to make shipping times as short as possible.

Amazon's initial seed funding came from Jeff Bezos's credit cards, savings, and a bank loan. In 1995, Kleiner, Perkins, Caufield and Byers (KPCB), a large and reputable VC firm, made a venture investment in Amazon. In 1997, a mere two years later, Amazon had a very successful initial public offering on the NASDAQ stock exchange.

In only three short years, Amazon went from idea to publicly traded company. Much like the many other publicly traded dot-com companies, Amazon had an incredibly successful run in the stock market. In the summer of 1999, the value of a single share of Amazon.com peaked at $106.68. By November 2, 2001, Amazon's stock price had fallen to $6.71, almost $100 below its all-time high.

KPCB were instrumental in helping Amazon grow from a seed-funded start-up to a mega-hot IPO candidate in two short years. KPCB's ability to provide both capital and guidance were critical in the success of Amazon. Most important perhaps was KPCB's willingness to adhere to Jeff Bezos's strategic plan to remain unprofitable for four to five years while building up the infrastructure, brand name, and reputation that would be needed for the company to succeed.

Although planning to lose money year after year seems to be a terrible strategy for any business, it was what made Amazon's success possible. At the time that Amazon was founded there were hordes of companies popping up almost every day. Most companies were promising profits immediately and were selling investors on the idea of overnight fortunes. There were so many companies making those kinds of promises that it became easy for investors to get swept up in the frenzy. Amazon stood out in that it promised to lose money every year for several years, and it promised that it would be a while before real sustainable profit would occur. This kind of realism and honesty was unusual and a key reason why KPCB agreed to invest in Amazon.com. At the peak of its share price in 1999, KPCB's stake in Amazon was worth well over one thousand times more than its initial investment.

Because of the investment KPCB made in Amazon, there is a total transformation in the way consumers shop today. Prices for most consumer goods have gone down, and the availability of previously hard-to-find items has gone up. Consumers now have the ability to research products, read reviews, compare prices, and make purchases all on one Web site. Amazon also revolutionized the way that people think about shipping and customer service. Products are delivered within days of the online purchase, and if unsatisfied, the consumer can send the product back free of charge.

In addition to the tangible benefits that Amazon provided, it also created an incredible amount of wealth in the form of jobs, new suppliers, and a slew of new service providers who participate in the Amazon product ecosystem. The total amount of consumer savings is in the billions of dollars. Today Amazon has branched out into dozens of other businesses and services and is continuing to stick to its initial philosophy of outstanding customer service.

PETS.COM

Pets.com has a similar story, except the ending is quite the opposite of Amazon's. Pets.com was founded by Greg McLemore in August 1998. The concept was to create a large online Web site to sell pet supplies at low prices and to deliver the products directly to the customer. Its business model was very similar in nature to Amazon's, which was even an investor. The first VC funding took place in 1999, and the other investors included Hummer Winblad Venture Partners and Bowman Capital Management.

Pets.com spent a lot of its venture funding on large warehouses and other shipment infrastructures, as well as on purchasing a competing Web-based pet supply company. It famously spent $1.2 million in January 2000 to buy an advertisement during the 2000 NFL Superbowl where it debuted its sock puppet spokesperson. In February 2000, Pets.com went public on the NASDAQ stock exchange, raising $82.5 million. The venture capitalists were able to get their money out of Pets.com at the time of the IPO.

Less than one year after going public, Pets.com went out of business, taking with it untold millions of dollars of investors' money. It left behind several massive distribution centers that it had constructed and left hundreds of employees out of work. Pets.com was one of many companies that were able to raise enormous sums of venture capital on an unproven business model, only to crash completely.

Pets.com spent a lot of their resources to build distribution facilities for customer transactions that they believed would happen at some point in the future. It spent hugely on

The Pets.com sock puppet mascot made its debut in a multimillion-dollar commercial during the 2000 Super Bowl. Since then, because of the demise of the company, it has become a symbol of the dot-com mania.

advertising and branding, instead of better management talent. Pets.com was attempting to ride the technology wave and to survive by playing the fund-raising game instead of focusing on building a well-managed and efficient organization.

Pets.com is a case study in the excesses of the dot-com bubble and the irrationality that can take place during a booming investment cycle.

The First Venture Capital Firm

The American Research and Development Corporation (ARDC) was the first modern venture capital firm. It was founded in 1946 by Georges Doriot, the former dean of Harvard Business School and the principal founder of INSEAD (Institut Européen d'Administration des Affaires) the leading business school in Europe.

ARDC was founded with the intent of funding businesses started by American soldiers returning from service in World War II. What defines ARDC as the first modern venture capital firm is that it raised its funds from the newly burgeoning institutional class of investors. This fund was a sign of things to come because it enabled new access to venture investment for people who were not part of the wealthiest tier of society.

ARDC is best remembered for its investment in DEC (Digital Equipment Corporation), which was at one time the leading high-tech company in the United States. It is reported that ARDC earned five hundred times its initial investment following the IPO of DEC.

Venture Capitalists as Chaperones

During the late 1990s, there was a lot of VC investing in similar technology businesses. Amazon.com and Pets.com effectively had the same business models, just with different products. Why was Amazon able to survive and Pets.com not? Most likely the biggest factors are operational in nature. The poor choices were not made by the Pets.com management team alone. The venture capitalists (Amazon, Hummer Winblad Venture Partners, and Bowman Capital Management) had board seats as part of their investment deal. They had a clear line of sight into the day-to-day operations of the company and should have clearly seen the warning signs of overspending and mismanagement.

Bill Gurley, a partner at Benchmark Capital, speaks at a technology conference in San Francisco. Venture capitalists' ability to network and promote is an important part of the value they bring to start-up companies.

The venture capitalists should have prevented the management team from spending so much money on warehouses and advertising and instead had it focus on building client relationships and finding ways to reduce costs.

DIVERSIFICATION OF RISK

One of the lessons that venture capital firms and venture investors have learned in the last two decades is that diversification is key to success. Diversification is the act of spreading your investments across several different companies, choosing to invest in companies that are not all in the same industry, and choosing to invest in companies that are seeking to sell to different markets. Diversification is a strategy that is used in all financial decision making in all sectors of financial services. It is not a new concept, but it is a new practice in the VC investing field.

VC firms and investors think about the companies they invest in as a portfolio. A portfolio is a group of investments that when looked at as a whole represents an average risk and reward profile. VC firms will usually have many different investments in many different start-ups at all times. This is important because it prevents the VC firm from "putting all its eggs in one basket," meaning that no single investment, if completely lost, would harm the VC firm to the point of failure.

VENTURE CAPITAL FUNDS

In addition to managing a portfolio of different venture investments, a VC firm will have different funds, each of which represents different outside investors and different start-up investments. VC firms get their money by creating funds that are designed to invest in start-ups based on a predetermined strategy.

VC firms will create a fund and then reach out to large investors, typically institutions such as insurance companies and pension funds, to raise money for the fund. There will be an agreement made with a contract, much like a venture capital agreement. The outside investor will invest its money in the

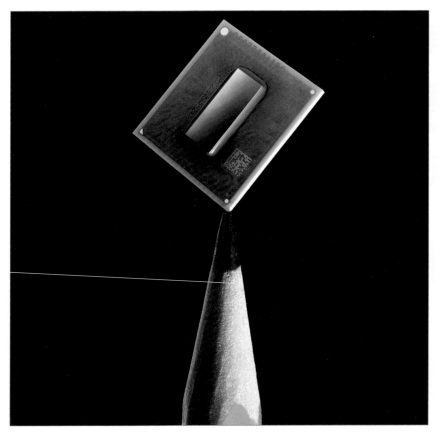

Microchips are one example of how venture capital can enable small and innovative individuals and companies to bring transformative products to the world.

fund created by the VC firm. The VC firm will then collect a fee based upon the total amount of money that it brings into the fund, usually 5 percent of the total amount of money in the fund each year, plus the VC will keep up to 20 percent of all profits from successful start-up investments.

The different funds that the VC firms create have fixed life spans, meaning they have a start and a stop date. When a fund reaches its end date it is closed, and any money that remains in the fund is returned to the outside investors.

SPECIALIZED VENTURE CAPITALISTS

Some VC firms will create special funds that have specific requirements for the kinds of start-ups they invest in. The fund could be dedicated to biotechnology, nanotechnology, or some other kind of industry, and it will only invest in start-ups that fit a very particular profile. This can be very attractive to outside investors who may have an interest in investing in companies that the fund is targeting.

Typically, VC firms are dedicated to only a few industry or technology types and will create funds that are focused on those few types. This practice allows VC firms to become expert in a particular field and to gain a lot of knowledge about the competition and direction within a specific industry.

CHAPTER FIVE

NONMONETARY BENEFITS

Venture capitalists play a vital role in scouting new technologies and bringing them to the market in a commercial product or service. This role is important because it turns scientific discovery into practically applied development. Venture capitalists don't participate in the scientific or development work, but they provide the resources that allow the start-up to create new products. This endeavor is very important to society because it is a role that is not duplicated in large corporate enterprise or government and rarely at university or collegiate institutions. Venture capital allows for innovation to be profitable.

ADVANCING TECHNOLOGICAL BREAKTHROUGHS

Because of the way that VC deals are structured, it is important for VCs to have investments in multiple ventures simultaneously. VCs must do this in order to diversify their portfolio risk. However, the unintended benefit it creates is a steady stream of investment in new companies and the creation of new products.

Large companies have a very hard time innovating and inventing new products. Large companies have complex internal structures, lots of employees, and many offices around the world. The environment of the large corporation is often not good for the creation of innovative new products and services.

Large corporations, just like schools and towns, develop a kind of culture and set of habits, which can often be counterproductive to the needs of a small start-up operation. Start-up companies also develop their own culture as they form. That culture is critical to the success of the company because it sets the tone for the entire team. If the team is not energized and passionate about the project, the likelihood of success diminishes.

Venture Debt

Venture debt is a loan that must be repaid within a fixed time period with interest. Venture debt is a viable alternative to venture capital for many firms today. Depending upon the start-up, some investors will offer venture debt instead of venture capital. Interest rates on venture debt can be very high due to the riskiness of the start-up. Although venture debt has a high interest component, it can be "cheaper" than venture capital because it does not participate in the exit of the company, which allows the start-up to keep more equity and thus reap greater benefits from a liquidity event.

Venture debt has been more popular in European nations where typical investors are more averse to risk than their American counterparts. Venture debt can be more appealing to investors because they receive annual debt service payments, which quickly reduce their total risk exposure.

Working with Large Corporations

Many large companies can create new innovations, but often those innovations are very similar to products and services that the large companies already produce. Procter & Gamble, a consumer products company, is very good at making new consumer products that are only slightly different from the ones it already makes. Procter & Gamble would have a very hard time creating an innovative start-up, such as a new Web-based social community like Facebook, because it requires a different discipline and mindset in all the members of the team. Procter & Gamble has all the resources needed to build something like Facebook, but it doesn't have the culture, expertise, or motivation to make such a product.

In the cycle of new product development, invention, and innovation, it is very common for large companies to scout for start-up companies with exciting new technologies for the purpose of buying the company and the technology. In this case, the large company gets to purchase a new technology it did not previously own, and it gets to avoid the difficulty of trying to manage internal start-up teams. Large companies can get so large that they have a difficult time changing course, and acquiring start-ups allows them to make course changes.

Not all large companies have difficulty with creating start-up companies. Some large companies create internal venture capital funds for the sole purpose of buying new companies and technologies. Some large companies will create incubator facilities, which allow for start-ups to form in isolation to escape the prevailing company culture. Some large companies are able to create start-up companies but will spin them out of the company as separate entities to allow the start-up to

Not all venture capital involves small start-ups. Large companies, such as Procter & Gamble, make venture investments in individual products and divisions within their businesses.

have room to grow. These various scenarios are all important to the overall venture capital industry.

The difference between a traditional venture capital firm and a corporate venture capital firm can be difficult to discern. However, the principles and goals are the same: invest in promising new teams and technologies in order to generate healthy returns on investment. However, the key difference between the two VC types is that the corporate VC will usually work toward investing in technologies and teams that will eventually become part of the corporation, whereas the traditional VC will work toward whatever liquidity event yields the greatest return on investment.

HELPING ENTREPRENEURS

The history of the venture capital industry and practice goes back many decades. Some would point to the earliest civilizations as proof that venture investors have always backed small

This statue of shipping and railroad tycoon Cornelius Vanderbilt stands as a reminder of the heights of financial success that an entrepreneur can achieve. Vanderbilt started his business with a single ferry boat and at one point was the wealthiest man in the United States.

players with big ideas. In terms of our recent history and current set of practices, the earliest records of VC activity go back to the middle of the twentieth century. During the early twentieth century, there were several wealthy families in the United States who controlled huge amounts of wealth. Families like the Roosevelts and the Vanderbilts controlled whole industries and had more wealth than could be spent in a lifetime. These wealthy families took to using their fortunes to provide financing for small companies with big ideas. These were the first modern venture investors.

For the first time, it was possible for a small company with limited resources to acquire large sums of capital for the purpose of business building, product research and development, and the creation of new commercial products. Previously the availability of start-up capital was limited, and the practice of lending was very rigid. The creation of the first venture funds that exploited the risk/reward ratio opened a whole new wave of companies seeking to get venture funding and made possible waves of new technological innovation.

THE TECHNOLOGICAL REVOLUTION OF THE TWENTIETH CENTURY

As mentioned earlier, the earliest venture investors in the twentieth century were wealthy private investors. These individual investors were able to exert much influence and control over their investments and the companies in which they invested. It was very difficult to gain an audience with these investors, so generally the companies that did gain funding were somehow connected to the investors and thus they had a pre-existing chance of getting funded, which discounted the merits of their

The baby boom generation of the post–World War II era was responsible for enormous economic growth and prosperity. The creation of new technologies and new industries during this time brought jobs and opportunity to the middle class.

ideas, preventing the escalation of truly innovate products that other start-ups could have developed.

After World War II, a shift in the venture investing world occurred. Companies that specialized in venture investing were formed. Unlike their wealthy individual predecessors, these new venture firms were receptive to any new idea or start-up venture, as long as the potential for success was real. Also unlike their predecessors, these new venture investors were not investing their own money. They were raising money in funds and then investing it.

CHAPTER SIX
THE GROWTH DILEMMA

There are times when a company grows too large to innovate. When this occurs, it sometimes acquires other companies to gain their innovations. This is true mostly for large and well established companies, like General Electric or Bocing. However, there are examples of newer companies that have grown from start-ups to large companies very quickly that also begin to use acquisition as a strategy for growth and innovation. The best example of this kind of rapid transformation from start-up to company acquirer is Google.

GOOGLE

During the first years of Google's growth, the company planned a very focused yet ambitious business plan to "organize the world's information." This goal was to take place on the Internet and included all forms of media from Web sites to online videos and even areas that were not yet part of the Internet, such as social relationships. In order to make this dream a reality, it would be necessary for Google to acquire many companies in order to add new technologies and capabilities that would be too difficult to duplicate for Google given its new large size. Google had grown so large that it was no longer able to operate like the lean start-up it hoped to remain.

The best example of Google's experience as a big company was their 2006 purchase of YouTube. YouTube today is a household name. It is the standard for online video distribution. Prior to purchasing YouTube, Google had a team dedicated to developing an internal product called Google Video, which was almost identical to YouTube but lacking in traffic and users. Google chose to purchase YouTube and to scrap its own Google Video project in order to take the clear lead in online video globally.

YouTube

YouTube was founded in February 2005 by three former PayPal employees: Chad Hurley, Steve Chen, and Jawed Karim. They received $11.5 million in venture funding from Sequoia Capital, a very well known and established VC firm based in San Francisco. The three founders led a small team and kept focused on developing the best product possible while ignoring the excesses of tech start-ups of the late 1990s.

YouTube launched in November 2005 and became an instant success. Within a short time it had millions of visitors and tens of thousands of videos posted on its site. Soon after, YouTube became the standard for online video sharing and viewing.

At roughly the same time that YouTube was developing its service, Google was hard at work making its own online video sharing service, Google Video. Google Video received a lukewarm response when it launched and never quite gained the traction in the market that had been hoped. The goal of Google Video was to allow Internet users to search for video in the same fashion that they searched for Web sites.

It became apparent very quickly that YouTube was the runaway leader in online video sharing, delivery, and search. Google decided to abandon its own platform and chose instead to pursue acquiring YouTube. In November 2006, one year after its launch, YouTube was purchased by Google for $1.65 billion.

Sequoia Capital far exceeded its own expectations with its investment in YouTube. Its return on investment requirements was dramatically exceeded, and the time frame from investment to

Showing gratitude for their entrepreneurial spirit, President Bill Clinton presents an award to YouTube founders Chad Hurley (*left*) and Steve Chen (*middle*) along with Google cofounder Larry Page.

Venture capital makes it possible for researchers to develop highly innovative new materials, which would otherwise be prohibitively expensive for a cash-strapped start-up to pursue.

exit was substantially shorter than is usually expected. YouTube could be viewed as the best possible investment scenario for a VC firm.

Sequoia Capital also perfectly performed its role as a provider of outside capabilities and network access. As we learned in the first chapter of this book, Sequoia Capital was an early investor in Google. It was able to provide a very strong networking connection between Google and YouTube, which enabled early communication between the two companies before any other outside party had the chance to step between them and hurt the chances of any possible deal. Sequoia had a very strong understanding of the culture and the management at both Google and YouTube, and it was able to foster a relationship between the two because of its prior experience working with both companies.

Microloans

The evolution of venture capital is happening today in the form of microloan corporations like the Grameen Bank, which makes small loans to entrepreneurs in developing countries. Loans are typically for less than a few hundred dollars and are used for purchasing things like livestock, computers, or a car, all of which can make an enormous difference for a start-up in a developing country.

The core premise of the Grameen Bank is that everyone has the potential to start a business and that given a chance they will work hard to be successful. What surprised most people about the success of the Grameen Bank is the incredibly high rate of loan repayment, which averages in the high 90 percent range. This is counterintuitive to western bankers who assume that poor people are less likely to repay their loans, but the data suggests that empowering the poor instills a sense of pride and dedication that results in a real desire to repay their debts.

Hopefully as our investment ecosystem continues to mature and evolve, we will see more innovative and equitable institutions like the Grameen Bank. There are seven billion people on this planet, and the majority don't have access to the upper echelons that make up our current VC system. Perhaps in time we will have many versions of the Grameen Bank funding microstart-ups around the world. Applying the same level of technology discovery to a population of hundreds of millions of start-ups may reveal ideas and visionaries that will far surpass our wildest dreams.

Venture capital and venture investors serve a vital role in our society. They enable new companies to bring new products and services to market, and those new products and services provide benefits to many people in society. Venture capital provides the impetus and focus that drives entrepreneurs to succeed. Venture capitalists offer outside influence and guidance. They also have a stake in the company and therefore have the incentive to see a successful and profitable outcome.

Venture capital helps turn scientific research into useful products that improve our lives. Much of our modern world was built on the technologies and products developed using venture funding. Hopefully we will continue to thrive based upon the continued efforts of start-ups and the venture capitalists who fund them.

GLOSSARY

angel investor An individual or a firm offering early stage investments to a start-up company in return for equity in the company.

board of directors A group, chosen by a company's shareholders, whose job is to supervise the company's management team to make sure that it is making the right decisions in protecting the shareholders' investment.

bootstrapping The act of starting a company using creativity and ingenuity to get all the things needed for very little money.

business plan A document that a start-up company will draft to describe the intent, goals, and projected financial model of the business.

dilution The process of reducing the relative percentage of shareholder ownership when additional shares are issued from a company.

diversification A financial principle that suggests that risk can be reduced if invested capital is spread around among numerous different investments.

due diligence The process of analyzing a company, its plan, its people, and its operations prior to making an investment.

entrepreneur A person who starts a new company.

equity A financial instrument that is used to specify ownership and financial interest in a company.

initial public offering (IPO) When a private company first offers shares of itself for sale on a public stock exchange.

institutional investor Someone who works for a very large financial fund, like a pension fund or an insurance company, who is charged with investing the capital of the fund to generate a return on investment.

liquidity event The financial transaction that allows the venture investors to get their invested capital out of the company. Also called an exit event.

portfolio A group of venture investments made by one VC, all active at the same time, that are considered to be an aggregate investment strategy designed to diversify and minimize risk.

return on investment (ROI) The amount of money that an investor earns on an investment.

shareholder Someone who owns shares in a company and therefore may own a claim to assets and cash-flow of the company.

FOR MORE INFORMATION

Community Development Venture Capital Alliance
    (CDVCA)
424 West 33rd Street, Suite 320
New York, NY 10001
(212) 594-6747
Web site: http://www.cdvca.org
The Community Development Venture Capital Alliance is a
    not-for-profit venture investment group that focuses on
    investing in economically disadvantaged communities
    and regions with the goal of yielding average rates of
    return. The mission of the fund is to promote the
    development of business and jobs while encouraging
    community-focused sustainability and corporate social
    responsibility.

European Private Equity and Venture Capital
    Association (EVCA)
Bastion Tower
Place du Champ de Mars 5
B-1050 Brussels
Belgium

+32 2 715 00 20

Web site: http://www.evca.eu

EVCA represents the interests of the VC industry
to regulators, develops professional standards,
provides industry research, provides professional
development and forums, and facilitates interaction
between its members and key industry participants,
including institutional investors, entrepreneurs,
policymakers, and academics. Its Web site is
packed with information about the European
VC world, which has some differences from the
U.S. VC industry.

Global Venture Capital and Private Equity Country
Attractiveness Index

IESE Business School - Barcelona Campus

Avenida Pearson, 21

08034 Barcelona

Spain

+34 93 253 42 00

Web site: http://blog.iese.edu/vcpeindex

This index, managed by faculty and researchers at the
IESE Business School in Barcelona Spain, is an
academic study of the conditions in countries around
the world. The Web site offers a free download of
detailed data about the assumptions and models used
to create the index.

Grameen Bank

Grameen Bank Bhaban

Mirpur - 2, Dhaka -1216
Bangladesh
(880-2) 8011138
Web site: http://www.grameen.com
The Grameen Bank is a microlending institution based
in India. Grameen makes microloans to Indian
entrepreneurs and existing small businesses that
would ordinarily not be able to secure any kind of
traditional bank loan.

National Venture Capital Association (NVCA)
1655 North Fort Myer Drive, Suite 850
Arlington, VA 22209
(70) 524-2549
Web site: http://www.nvca.org
The NVCA is a trade association dedicated to the
venture capital industry. It serves to provide
increased communication between individuals
employed in the venture capital industry, a
dvocacy for policies that foster the growth of
innovation, and education to the general public
about the venture capital industry. The NVCA
also provides a range of professional services
for its members.

Young Entrepreneur
8 West 38th Street, #1103
New York, NY, 10018
(212) 563-8080
Web site: http://www.youngentrepreneur.com

Young Entrepreneur is dedicated to providing education, information, and networking for young entrepreneurs who are working to launch or grow their start-up businesses. The site is filled with videos, articles, links, and information to help you learn more about being an entrepreneur.

Web Sites

Due to the changing nature of Internet links, Rosen Publishing has developed an online list of Web sites related to the subject of this book. This site is updated regularly. Please use this link to access the list:

http://www.rosenlinks.com/rwe/vent

FOR FURTHER READING

Chou, Scott. *Maxims, Morals, and Metaphors: A Philosophical Guide to Venture Capital.* Salt Lake City, UT: Aardvark Global Publishing, 2006.

Christen, Carol, and Richard N. Bolles. *What Color Is Your Parachute? For Teens.* Berkeley, CA: Ten Speed Press, 2010.

Collins, Robyn, and Kimberly Burleson Spinks. *Prepare to Be a Teen Millionaire.* Deerfield Beach, FL: HCI Publishing, 2008.

Gillespie-Brown, Jon. *So You Want to Be an Entrepreneur: How to Decide If Starting a Business Is Really for You.* Chichester, England: Capstone Publishing, Ltd. 2008.

Kiyosaki, Robert T. *Rich Dad, Poor Dad for Teens: The Secrets About Money—That You Don't Learn in School!* New York, NY: Warner Books/Little, Brown, 2009.

Rankin, Kenrya, and Eriko Takada. *Start It Up: The Complete Teen Business Guide to Turning Your Passions into Pay.* San Francisco, CA: Zest Books/Orange Avenue Publishing, 2011.

Simmons, Raie. *Entrepreneurship* (Junior Library of Money). Broomall, PA: Mason Crest Publishers, 2009.

Stokes, Carol. *Basic Beginnings: A Finance Management Handbook for Teens and Young Adults.* Seattle, WA: Amazon Digital Services, 2010.

Swartz, Jon. *Young Wealth: Trade Secrets from Teens Who Are Changing American Business*. Bloomington, IN: Rooftop Publishing, 2006.

Urquhart-Brown, Susan. *The Accidental Entrepreneur: The 50 Things I Wish Someone Had Told Me About Starting a Business*. New York, NY: AMACOM Books, 2008.

White, James Timothy. *Born to Be Business Savvy: 31 Essential Tips from the Kid Millionaire on a Personal Journey*. New York, NY: Morgan James Publishing, 2010.

Wilson Solovic, Susan. *The Girls' Guide to Building a Million-Dollar Business*. New York, NY: AMACOM Books, 2007.

BIBLIOGRAPHY

Ante, Spencer E. *Creative Capital*. Boston, MA: Harvard Business Press, 2008.

Awe, Susan C. *The Entrepreneur's Information Sourcebook*. Westport, CT: Libraries Unlimited, 2006.

Cumming, Douglas. *Venture Capital: Investment Strategies, Structures, and Policies* (Robert W. Kolb Series). Hoboken, NJ: John Wiley & Sons, 2010.

Draper, William H., and Eric Schmidt. *The Startup Game: Inside the Partnership Between Venture Capitalists and Entrepreneurs*. New York, NY: Palgrave MacMillan, 2011.

Gladstone, Laura, and David Gladstone. *Venture Capital Investing: The Complete Handbook for Investing in Private Businesses for Outstanding Profits*. New York, NY: Prentice Hall, 2004.

Gompers, Paul, and Josh Lerner. *The Venture Capital Cycle*. Cambridge, MA: MIT Press, 2006.

Hardymon, Felda, Ann Leamon, and Josh Lerner. *Venture Capital and Private Equity: A Case Book*. Hoboken, NJ: John Wiley & Sons, 2009.

Kizer, Jared, and Larry E. Swedroe. *Alternative Investments*. New York, NY: Bloomberg Press, 2008.

Klonowski, Darek. *The Venture Capital Investment Process.* New York, NY: Palgrave MacMillan, 2010.

Mahagaonkar, Prashanth. *Money and Ideas: Four Studies on Finance, Innovation and the Business Life Cycle.* New York, NY: Springer, 2010.

Metrick, Andrew, and Ayako Yasuda. *Venture Capital and the Finance of Innovation.* Hoboken, NJ: John Wiley & Sons, 2010.

INDEX

About the Author

Peter K. Ryan earned his B.A. at Villanova University and M.B.A. from the Lally School of Management and Technology at Rensselaer Polytechnic Institute. He began his professional life working at the New York Stock Exchange and American Stock Exchange.

Photo Credits

Cover, p. 17 Shutterstock.com, cover (headline) © www.istockphoto.com/ Lilli Day; pp. 5, 10 Bloomberg/Bloomberg via Getty Images; pp. 7, 16, 30, 40, 51, 60 Mario Tama/Getty Images; p. 12 © www.istockphoto.com/ Dan Bachman; p. 14 John MacDougal/AFP/Getty Images; p. 19 Gabriela Hasbun/Redux; pp. 22–23 © AP Images; pp. 24–25 Dan Krauss/Getty Images; p. 27 Getty Images; p. 31 Erik Snyder/Photodisc/Thinkstock; p. 33 AFP/AFP/Getty Images; pp. 35, 54–55 © AP Images; pp. 36–37, 62–63 Chris Hondros/Getty Images; p. 41 Paul Souders/Getty Images; p. 45 Scott Gries/Getty Images; p. 47 Bloomberg/Bloomberg via Getty Images; p. 49 Steve Bornstein/Stone/Getty Images; p. 56 Max Alexander/Dorling Kindersley/Getty Images; p. 56 Max Alexander/ Dorling Kindersley/ Getty Images; pp. 58–59 Van D. Bucher/Photo Researchers/Getty Images; pp. 64–65 U. Bellhaeuser/ScienceFoto/Getty Images; cover and interior graphic elements: © www.istockphoto.com/Andrey Prokhorov (front cover), © www.istockphoto.com/Dean Turner (back cover and interior pages), © www.istockphoto.com/Darja Tokranova (39); © www. itockphoto.com/articular (p. 46); © www.istockphoto.com/studiovision (pp. 68, 70, 74, 76, 78); © www.istockphoto.com/Chen Fu Soh (multiple interior pages).

Designer: Nicole Russo; Editor: Nicholas Croce;
Photo Researcher: Marty Levick